Copyright© 2018 by Dirty Girl Cookbooks

ALL RIGHTS RESERVED. By purchase of this book, you have been licensed one copy for personal use only. No part of this work may be reproduced, redistributed, or used in any form or by any means without prior written permission of the publisher and copyright owner.

TABLE OF CONTENTS

BREAKFAST

High Protein Egg Muffins	4
Stuffed Avocado	5
Zucchini Cheese Muffins	6

SAUCES

Garlic Dressing	7
Avocado Ranch Dressing	8
Spicy Mayo Sauce	9
Ranch Dressing	10
Cauliflower Puree	11

SIDES

Guacamole Deviled Eggs	12
Roasted Buffalo Garlic Cauliflower	13
Keto White Bread	14
Roasted Garlic Broccoli Cauliflower Mash	15
Cauliflower Rice	16

MAIN COURSE

Grilled Salmon with Cauliflower Puree	17
Cauliflower Risotto	18
Spinach and Cream Cheese Stuffed Chicken Wrapped in Bacon	19
Zucchini Mac N' Cheese	20
Crack Beef Slaw	21
Swedish Meatballs	22
Chicken Cabbage Enchiladas	23
Chicken Bacon Ranch Casserole	25
Sesame Chicken with Broccoli	26
Thai Coconut Curry Chicken	27
Broccoli and Cheese Soup	28
Loaded Zucchini Boats	29
Buffalo Chicken Meatballs	30
Chicken and Cheese Stuffed Red Peppers	31
Creamy Sun-Dried Tomato Chicken	32
Pecan Crusted Fish Fillet	33
Coconut Shrimp	34
Almond Crusted Chicken	35
Avocado Pecan Chicken Salad	36
Egg Roll in a Bowl	37
Fried Parmesan Tomatoes	38
Braised Cabbage & Sausage	39

DESSERTS

Pumpkin Spice Fat Bombs	40
Cream Cheese Peanut Butter Fat Bomb	41
Pecan Cheesecake Fat Bomb Muffins	42
Peanut Butter Almond Cookies	43
No-Bake Peanut Butter Caramel Cookies	44
Sausage Puff Keto Fat Bomb	45

Breakfast

HIGH PROTEIN EGG MUFFINS

The great thing about these muffins is you can choose to use many varieties of vegetables. For example, if you like your eggs spicier, feel free to add some jalapeño peppers. If you prefer tomatoes, substitute one of the below vegetables for ½ cup of tomatoes.

INGREDIENTS:

- 1 Dozen Eggs
- 3 Strips of Bacon
- ¾ Cup Diced Mushrooms
- ½ Cup Diced Bell Peppers
- ½ Cup Diced Onions
- ½ Cup Diced Broccoli (No Stems)
- ½ Cup Chopped Raw Spinach
- ½ Cup Heavy Cream
- 1 Cup Shredded Parmesan Cheese
- ¼ Cup Whole Milk
- Sea Salt & Black Pepper

INSTRUCTIONS:

Preheat your oven to 375 °F.

Mix all diced vegetables in one bowl and then scoop into muffin tin spreading evenly. Add salt & pepper to each cup as desired.

Chop bacon into bite-size pieces and add to each muffin cup.

Beat eggs, heavy cream, milk, salt, and pepper until mixed well. Pour evenly over vegetables in the muffin tin.

Spread Parmesan cheese evenly into each muffin cup.

Stir each muffin cup until all ingredients are mixed well.

Place muffin tin in the preheated oven for 20 minutes.

Bon Appétit!

Breakfast

STUFFED AVOCADO

INGREDIENTS:

- Avocado
- 2 Eggs
- 4 Slices of Bacon
- Option to Include Diced Vegetables
  (Onions, Spinach, Mushrooms, Peppers, Jalapeño)
- Sea Salt and Black Pepper

INSTRUCTIONS:

Preheat oven to 425°F.

Slice your avocado in half and remove the pit. Place halves in cast iron pan.

Crack an egg inside and top with desired vegetables.

Sprinkle with salt and pepper.

Place strips of bacon in the shape of an X on top.

Cook until eggs are cooked to your liking.

Bon Appétit!

Breakfast

ZUCCHINI CHEESE MUFFINS

INGREDIENTS:

- 3 Cups Grated Zucchini
- ½ Cup Butter, Melted
- 10 Eggs
- 2 Tbsp. Oregano
- ¾ Cup Coconut Flour
- 1 Cup Cheddar Cheese, Shredded
- ½ Cup Goat Cheese, Crumbled
- ½ Tsp. Baking Powder
- 1 Cup Heavy Cream

INSTRUCTIONS:

What's so great about this recipe is the simplicity of it.

Begin by preheating the oven to 375°F.

Next, remove any remaining water from the grated zucchini. Do this by wrapping the zucchini in paper towels and squeezing it.

In a mixing bowl, beat the eggs until scrambled.

Add butter, oregano, flour, cream, and baking powder.

Pour eggs into greased muffin tin and evenly distribute zucchini and then top with cheddar and goat cheese.

Cook in the oven for 25 minutes.
Muffins should be easy to remove from tin.

Bon Appétit!

Sauces

GARLIC DRESSING

INGREDIENTS:

- 6 Garlic Cloves
- ½ Cup Apple Cider Vinegar
- 1 Cup Olive Oil
- 1 Tbsp. Dijon Mustard
- ½ Cup Parmesan Cheese, Grated
- ¼ Cup Heavy Cream
- Sea Salt and Black Pepper
- ½ Tsp. Onion Powder
- 2 Tbsp. Fresh Parsley, Chopped

INSTRUCTIONS:

In a blender, blend all ingredients except Parmesan cheese. Add salt and pepper to taste.

Add Parmesan cheese and mix by hand.

Transfer to a container with an airtight lid.

Refrigerate when not using.

Bon Appétit!

Sauces

AVOCADO RANCH DRESSING

INGREDIENTS:

- 1 Avocado, Pitted
- 1 Garlic Clove, Minced
- ¼ Cup Cilantro, Chopped
- ¼ Cup Sour Cream
- 1 Tbsp. Fresh Lemon Juice
- 1 Tbsp. Fresh Dill, Chopped
- ½ Tsp. Onion Powder
- 3 Tbsp. Olive Oil
- Sea Salt and Black Pepper

INSTRUCTIONS:

Process all ingredients in a food processor and package in a glass jar (such as a mason jar) with a lid.

Refrigerate.

Bon Appétit!

Sauces

SPICY MAYO SAUCE

INGREDIENTS:

- 1/3 Cup Mayonnaise
- 1 Tsp. Sriracha
- 1 Tbsp. Garlic Chili Sauce
- 1 Tsp. Swerve (Sweetener)
- 1 Pinch of Sea Salt

INSTRUCTIONS:

Mix all ingredients in a glass jar or airtight sealed container.

Serve chilled or warm!

Bon Appétit!

Sauces

RANCH DRESSING

INGREDIENTS:

- ½ Cup Sour Cream
- ¼ Cup Heavy Cream
- 2 Tbsp. White Distilled Vinegar or Fresh Lemon Juice
- 2 Cloves Garlic, Minced
- 2 Tbsp. Dill Weed, Chopped
- 1 Tbsp. Parsley, Chopped
- 1 Tsp. Fresh Chives
- 1 Tsp. Onion Powder
- Sea Salt and Black Pepper to Taste

INSTRUCTIONS:

Now for the easy part – mix all ingredients (in a mason jar if you have one), cover with a lid and keep refrigerated.

Bon Appétit!

Sauces

CAULIFLOWER PUREE

INGREDIENTS:

- 1 Head of Cauliflower
- 2 Garlic Cloves, Minced
- 4 Tbsp. Butter
- ¼ Onion, Sliced
- 1/3 Cup Heavy Whipping Cream
- 1 Cup Chicken Stock
- ¼ Cup Sour Cream
- 2 Tbsp. Parmesan
- Sea Salt and Black Pepper, to Taste

INSTRUCTIONS:

To start bring a medium pot of water with 1 teaspoon of salt to boil.

Chop stems off cauliflower and separate into florets. Place in boiling water. Cook until tender (a fork will easily go into the cauliflower once it is cooked enough).

While cauliflower is cooking sauté the minced garlic and onions in the butter. Cook until golden brown.

Placed drained cauliflower, onions, garlic, chicken stock, and heavy cream into a blender. Blend until smooth. Add sour cream and Parmesan and continue blending. Taste and add salt and pepper as needed.

Consistency should be thin – if needed add more chicken stock, heavy cream and sour cream until the thickness is that of a puree.

Bon Appétit!

Sides

GUACAMOLE DEVILED EGGS

INGREDIENTS:

- 6 Hard Boiled Eggs
- 2 Avocados (Pitted)
- 1 Tbsp. Sour Cream
- 1 Tbsp. Lime Juice
- 1 Tbsp. Lemon Juice
- ½ Small Tomato, Diced Finely
- 2 Tbsp. Diced White Oonion
- 1 Tbsp. Olive Oil
- ¼ Cup Cilantro, Finely Chopped
- 1 Serrano Chile Pepper, Minced
- 1 Tsp. Paprika

INSTRUCTIONS:

Peel your hard-boiled eggs. Remove the egg yolk and set aside. Cut the egg whites in half lengthwise.

Scoop the avocado out of their skins and place in a bowl. Mash with a fork.

Take 3 of the egg yolks and add to avocado mush.

Add sour cream, tomato, onion, cilantro, chile, olive oil, lemon juice, and lime juice.

Add salt and pepper to taste.

Scoop spoonful of avocado mixture into each hard-boiled egg. Top with additional cilantro and paprika.

Bon Appétit!

Sides

ROASTED BUFFALO GARLIC CAULIFLOWER

INGREDIENTS:

- 1 Medium Sized Head of Cauliflower (Florets)
- 1 Egg
- 1 Cup Almond Flour
- ½ Cup Buffalo Sauce
- ¼ Cup Butter, Melted
- 1 Tbsp. Lemon Juice
- Sea Salt and Black Pepper, to Taste

INSTRUCTIONS:

Preheat oven to 450°F.

Begin by beating the egg in a small bowl.

Pour the almond flour into a separate small bowl.

Pour the butter, lemon juice and buffalo sauce in a ziploc gallon bag.

Dip each cauliflower into the egg and then into the flour.

Once breaded, place in buffalo sauce.

You will want to have all cauliflower in the ziploc.

Add salt and pepper and then shake the ziploc until all cauliflower is covered.

Place buffalo cauliflower on a pre-greased baking pan and cook in the oven for 15-20 minutes or until cauliflower begins to brown.

Serve with Keto ranch dressing (Pg. 10)

Bon Appétit!

Sides

KETO WHITE BREAD

INSTRUCTIONS:

- 1 Cup Almond Flour (Super Finely Ground)
- ¼ Cup Coconut Flour
- 2 Tsp. Baking Powder
- 2 Tsp. Active Dry Yeast
- 2 Tsp. Honey
- 1/2 Cup Water (Luke Warm)
- ¼ Tsp. Sea Salt
- 1/2 Cup Butter
- 2 Tbsp. Coconut Oil
- 6 Eggs (Room Temperature)
- 3 Tbsp. Swerve (Sweetner)
- ¼ Tsp. Xanthan Gum

INGREDIENTS:

Preheat oven to 355°F.

Prepare your bread pan with parchment or baking paper.

In a small bowl, beat the eggs.

In a small saucepan, heat the butter on the stovetop. Once the butter is melted add the coconut oil. Mix the two together.

In a bowl, add the yeast, honey and water. Cover with towel and allow for yeast to activate (6-7 minutes).

In a separate mixing bowl, mix the almond flour, coconut flour, baking powder, swerve and salt.

Once the yeast is proofed, add in the eggs/coconut mix into one bowl.

Continue mixing and add in the flour mixture. Mix with an electric mixer.

Pour into prepared bread pan.

Place bread in oven for approximately 45 minutes. Check that bread is completely cooked by sticking a toothpick in the middle.

Bon Appétit!

Sides

ROASTED GARLIC AND BROCCOLI CAULIFLOWER MASH

INGREDIENTS:

- 4 Tbsp. Butter
- 2 Cloves Garlic (Minced)
- ½ Cup Sliced Onions
- ½ Lb. Chopped Broccoli (No Stems)
- 1 Lb. Cauliflower
- ¼ Cup Heavy Cream
- 1 Cup Whole Milk
- 4 Oz. Cream Cheese
- ½ Cup Sour Cream
- ½ Cup Shredded Parmesan Cheese
- Sea Salt and Black Pepper

INSTRUCTIONS:

First, begin by bringing a pot of water and 1 teaspoon of salt to a boil. Add cauliflower and cook until a fork easily slides into the cauliflower.

While cauliflower is cooking, melt 2 tbsp. of the butter in a saucepan. Add onions and garlic. Cook until onions and garlic are brown and beginning to caramelize. Add broccoli and 1-teaspoon salt and pepper.

Pour onions, garlic, broccoli, heavy cream, ½ cup milk, cream cheese, and cooked cauliflower into a blender. Blend until smooth.

Pour mixture back into the same saucepan that was used to sauté onions, garlic, and broccoli.

Add sour cream and remaining 2 tbsp. butter, ½ cup milk, ½ cup parmesan cheese, and ½ cup sour cream. Consistency should be that of a mash versus a puree.

Sea salt and black pepper, to taste.

Bon Appétit!

Sides

CAULIFLOWER RICE

INGREDIENTS:

- 2 Heads Cauliflower, Cut Into Florets
- 6 Tbs. Butter
- 4 Garlic Cloves, Minced
- 2 Tbsp. Lemon Juice
- 2 Tbsp. Parsley, Chopped

INSTRUCTIONS:

Place cauliflower in a food processor and pulse until the cauliflower resembles that of rice.

Add butter, garlic and lemon juice to a large skillet and heat on medium-high.

Add cauliflower, parsley, salt, and pepper.

Cook cauliflower until it softens (5-6 minutes).

Remove and serve.

Bon Appétit!

Main Course

GRILLED SALMON WITH CAULIFLOWER PUREE

INGREDIENTS: GRILLED SALMON

- 1 Pound Fresh Boneless Salmon Fillet, Skinned (Except for the Bottom) and Cut Into 4 (4-Ounce) Pieces
- 1 ½ tbsp. Olive Oil
- 1 Lemon
- Sea Salt & Black Pepper, to Taste
- 1 Tbsp. Dried or Fresh Chopped Thyme

First, begin by preheating the oven to 450°F.

Cover the salmon in olive oil and fresh-squeezed lemon juice.

Next sprinkle the thyme, salt, and pepper evenly over the salmon fillets.

Place fillets in a glass pan uncovered in the oven for 20 minutes.

CAULIFLOWER PUREE
(Pg. 11)

INGREDIENTS: SPINACH

- 8 oz. Fresh Spinach (Washed and Dried)
- Sea Salt and Black Pepper, to Taste

Place some of the spinach in a sauté pan on the stove over medium heat.

Continue adding more spinach as it begins to cook down. Gently toss the spinach so that it cooks evenly.

After it is finished cooking you may choose to pat it down with a towel or napkin to remove some of the extra cooked juices.

PLATING YOUR DISH:

Start by placing the cooked spinach on the center of your plate. Next, place a piece of salmon on top of the bed of spinach. Finally, pour a few tablespoons of the cauliflower puree on top of the salmon. If needed, sprinkle with a bit of salt and pepper to complete.

Bon Appétit!

Main Course

CAULIFLOWER RISOTTO

INGREDIENTS:

- 1 Head of Cauliflower (Food Processed or Blended Into Cauliflower Rice)
- 1 Cup Vegetable Stock
- 1 ½ Cup Chopped Portobello or Another Type of Mushroom
- 2 Cloves Garlic (Minced)
- 2 Tbsp. Butter
- 1 Cup Heavy Cream or Coconut Milk
- ¾ Cup White Wine
- ½ Cup Shredded Parmesan Cheese
- Sea Salt and Black Pepper, to Taste
- 1 Tbsp. Fresh Rosemary and/or Thyme
- 1 Tbsp. Basil Pesto (Optional)

INSTRUCTIONS:

Begin by preheating the oven to 415°F.

Take a large skillet and add butter while on high heat. Add garlic, salt, and pepper. Cook until golden brown.

Add Portobello mushroom. Coat the mushroom in the butter sauce and cook until the mushroom begins to absorb the butter.

Add cauliflower rice and cook for 2-3 minutes, stirring frequently.

Pour in heavy cream (or coconut milk), vegetable stock, ¾ of the cheese and most of the white wine. Bring to a simmer then reduce the heat and place the lid on top cooking for 15 minutes, until the sauce thickens.

Add remaining wine, Parmesan cheese, fresh rosemary/thyme, salt, and pepper to taste.

Option to add basil pesto if you would like a pesto cauliflower risotto.

Bon Appétit!

Main Course

SPINACH AND CREAM CHEESE STUFFED CHICKEN WRAPPED IN BACON

INGREDIENTS:

- 2 Lb. Boneless Chicken Breasts (4-8 oz. Pieces)
- 6 Oz. Raw Bacon (About 8 Strips)
- 1 Cup Chopped Spinach
- 4 Tbsp. Full Fat Cream Cheese
- Sea Salt and Black Pepper

INSTRUCTIONS:

Begin by preheating your oven to 375°F.

Flatten the chicken with a meat mallet.

Next, you will need to butterfly the chicken breasts. Begin by placing your hand on top of the chicken. It helps to use a sharp knife to slice the breast in half. Slice it almost all the way through so that you end up with the chicken resembling a butterfly when open.

Sea salt and black pepper the inside and outside of the chicken.

Take ¼ cup of the chopped spinach and 1 tablespoon of cream cheese and spread evenly on the flaps of the chicken. Fold in half so that the chicken is back to its original breast.

Wrap 2 pieces of bacon around each chicken breast so that you fully wrap the chicken breast.

Place in preheated oven for 30-35 minutes or until bacon is fully cooked. Cream cheese may be oozing out.

Option to serve with Cauliflower Puree for a delicious addition.

Bon Appétit!

Main Course

ZUCCHINI MAC N' CHEESE

INGREDIENTS:

- 2 Tbsp. Bacon Grease
- 2 Tbsp. Avocado Oil
- 2 Cups Mild Goat Milk Cheddar Cheese
- 1 Sweet Onion, Sliced
- 2 Zucchinis, Sliced
- ½ Cup Vegetable Stock
- 1/2 Tsp. Dijon Mustard
- 6 Oz. Sharp Cheddar Cheese, Shredded
- 6 Oz. Parmesan Cheese, Shredded
- 2 Cloves Garlic, Minced
- 4 Tbsp. Whole Milk
- 4 Oz. Full Fat Cream Cheese
- Sea Salt and Black Pepper, to Taste

INSTRUCTIONS:

Heat bacon grease in a large skillet on medium heat. Add garlic and onion; cook until translucent.

Add sliced zucchini, salt, and pepper. Stir occasionally until zucchini and onions begin to brown.

Set cooked vegetables aside.

In the same large skillet heat the vegetable stock on medium heat.

Add cream cheese and milk to skillet and begin adding shredded cheddar and Parmesan cheeses. As the mixture begins to melt continue adding cheese until all is melted.

Add Dijon mustard, goat cheese, salt, and pepper.

Add vegetables to the melted cheese mixture.

Coat a baking dish with avocado oil and pour mixture into dish. Sprinkle with additional desired salt and pepper.

Place in the broiler on high for 5 minutes or until cheese begins to brown on top.

Bon Appétit!

Main Course

CRACK BEEF SLAW

INGREDIENTS:

- 1 Head Purple Cabbage (Leaves Shredded)
- 3 Carrots, Peeled and Shredded
- 1 Red Onion, Peeled and Sliced Thinly
- 2 Cloves Garlic
- 2 Tbsp. Sesame Seed Oil
- 1 Lb. Ground Beef
- ½ White Onion, Diced
- Slaw Mix
- 1 Tbsp. Sriracha
- 2 Tbsp. Coconut Aminos
- 1 Tbsp. Vinegar
- Sea Salt and Black Pepper, to Taste
- 1 Tbsp. Sesame Seeds
- 1 Stalk Green Onion (Chopped)

INSTRUCTIONS:

Begin by creating your slaw mix by combining the shredded purple cabbage, carrots and thinly sliced red onion.

Cook ground beef with diced onion, garlic, salt, and pepper.

Remove ground beef from pan and drain juice.

In the same pan heat up sesame oil, add in the slaw mix and cook to desired tenderness.

Stir in coconut aminos, Sriracha, vinegar and add meat back in.

Top with sesame seeds, green onions, salt, and pepper to taste.

Bon Appétit!

Main Course

SWEDISH MEATBALLS

INGREDIENTS:

- 1 Lb. Ground Pork
- 1 Lb. Ground Beef
- 1 White Onion, Diced
- 1 Cup Grated Zucchini (Keep Water)
- 1 Egg
- 1 Tsp. All-Purpose Seasoning
- Sea Salt and Pepper, to Taste
- 2 Tbsp. Butter
- 1 Cup Chicken Broth
- 1 Tbsp. Dijon Mustard
- ¾ Cup Heavy Cream
- 2 Oz. Cream Cheese
- 1 Tbsp. Chopped Parsley (for Garnish)

INSTRUCTIONS:

Combine ground meat, shredded zucchini (with water), diced onion, egg and salt into a medium-size bowl. Mix with hands. Over mixing will cause meatballs to be less tender when cooked.

Melt butter into a large cast iron skillet.

Roll meat mixture into small round meatballs. Use an ice cream scoop for easy measuring.

Cook meatballs in skillet until each side is browned.

Combine heavy cream, cream cheese, mustard, and broth.

Pour cream sauce into skillet with meatballs and bring to a simmer. Cook until meatballs are cooked thoroughly and the sauce has thickened.

Sprinkle with parsley and serve.

Bon Appétit!

Main Course

CHICKEN CABBAGE ENCHILADAS

INGREDIENTS:

ENCHILADA SAUCE
- 1 Tbsp. Avocado Oil
- 2 Garlic Cloves (Minced)
- 2 Cups Plain Tomato Sauce
- ½ Tsp. Ancho Chili Powder

ENCHILADA FILING
- 1 Head Green Cabbage
- 1 Tbsp. Avocado Oil
- 1 ½ Lb. Chicken (Cooked and Shredded)
- 2 Clove Garlic (Minced)
- 1-4 Oz. Can Diced Green Chiles
- 1 Tbsp. Adobo Sauce
- ½ White Onion (Diced)
- ¼ Tsp. Cumin

TOPPINGS
- 2 Tbsp. Chopped Cilantro
- 1 Cup Shredded Monterey Jack Cheese
- 1 Cup Shredded Cheddar Cheese
- ½ Cup Sour Cream
- ½ Cup Diced Tomatoes
- ½ Cup Diced Avocado
- ¼ Cup Chopped Jalapeño Peppers (Optional For Extra Spice)

INSTRUCTIONS:

PREPARING THE ENCHILADA SHELLS

Prepare the cabbage by cutting off the stem and removing the leaves one by one. Be careful not to tear the leaves in the process.

Boil a pot of water and place the cabbage leaves in the water for 1 minute. Place the leaves in cold water immediately after removing them from the boiling water. Remove from the cold water after 20 seconds and then place on a towel to dry.

Preheat oven to 375°F.

ENCHILADA FILLING:

In a large saucepan heat avocado oil. Add diced onions and cook until sautéed. Add garlic.

Add chicken, green chiles, adobo sauce, cumin, salt, and pepper. Sauté for 3-4 minutes. Remove and set aside.

ENCHILADA SAUCE:

Heat avocado oil. Add minced garlic and cook. Add tomato sauce and chili powder. Stir and set aside.

ASSEMBLING ENCHILADAS:

Lay out the dry cabbage leaves and spread chicken mixture in the middle of each on.

Top chicken mixture with 1 tbsp. of each cheese (Monterey and cheddar).

Fold cabbage and place seam down in baking dish. Repeat for remaining leaves (until all mixture is used).

Pour enchilada sauce on top of all cabbage rolls.

Top with remaining cheese and cook in the oven uncovered for 25 minutes.

Garnish with cilantro, diced tomatoes, avocados and salt, and pepper.

Bon Appétit!

Main Course

CHICKEN BACON RANCH CASSEROLE

INGREDIENTS:

- 1 Lb. Cooked Chicken (Chopped Into Bite-Size Pieces)
- 2 Tbsp. Butter
- 1 ½ Tablespoons of Ranch Seasoning Mix (About Half a Packet)
- ¼ Cup Heavy Cream
- 2/3 Cup Reduced Sodium Chicken Broth
- 8 Oz. Cream Cheese
- 8 Oz. Shredded Cheddar Cheese
- 1/3 Cup Cooked Bacon Crumbs
- 1 Lb. Steamed Broccoli (Chopped Into Bite-Size Pieces)
- 1 Tbsp. Minced Onion
- 1 Tsp. Garlic Powder
- Sea Salt and Black Pepper, to Taste
- Green Onion Stalk (for Garnish)

INSTRUCTIONS:

Preheat oven to 350°F.

In a skillet heat the butter, cream cheese, ranch mix, chicken broth, heavy cream, and spices. Mix well.

Add chicken, broccoli, ¾ of the cheese and ¼ cup of bacon crumbles and mix together. Add salt and pepper.

Pour mixture into a baking dish that has been coated with avocado oil. Sprinkle remaining cheese and bacon on top.

Bake for approximately 35 minutes (since nothing is raw – you are just cooking to heat all ingredients).

Garnish with green onion and add salt and pepper to taste.

Bon Appétit!

Main Course

SESAME CHICKEN WITH BROCCOLI

INGREDIENTS:

- 1 Lb. Chicken, Cubed
- 1 Egg
- ½ Tsp. Guar Gum Powder
- 1 Tbsp. Avocado Oil
- 12 Ounces Broccoli Florets (Steamed)
- ¼ Cup Coconut Aminos
- 1 Tsp. Sesame Oil
- 1 ½ Tsp. Arrowroot Powder
- 1 Clove Garlic (Minced)
- 2 Tbsp. Sesame Seeds
- Red Pepper Flakes, to Taste
- ¼ Cup Chopped Green Onion
- 2 Tbsp. Monk Fruit Sweetener
- 2 Cups Cauliflower Rice (Cooked)

INSTRUCTIONS:

Begin by mixing the Guar Gum powder with the egg. Stir vigorously until the mixture becomes a thick white foam. This allows for a thick coating that will give your chicken the "breading" of the sesame chicken you are probably accustomed to.

Toss chicken in mixture until fully coated.

Add salt and pepper.

In a large pan, heat the avocado oil and add minced garlic.

Next, begin "frying" the chicken. The chicken should end up with a brown coating.

In a separate pan, begin to heat the coconut aminos, sesame oil, arrowroot powder, sesame seeds, Monk fruit sweetener, and red pepper flakes.

Remove the chicken one by one from the frying pan and place in the sesame mixture. Toss until fully coated.

Next, you will need to prepare your broccoli. Steam in the microwave or on the stovetop.

Finally, combine the broccoli with the sesame chicken (using the pan from the sesame mixture).

Serve over cauliflower rice and garnish with chopped green onion.

Bon Appétit!

Main Course

THAI COCONUT CURRY CHICKEN

INGREDIENTS:

- 1 ½ Lb. Chicken Breasts (or Thighs)
- 2 Tbsp. Coconut Oil
- 2 Tbsp. Fish Sauce
- 1 Can- 13 Oz. Coconut Cream
- 4 Tsp. Red Curry Paste
- 1 Zucchini (Cut Into ½" X 2" Spears)
- 1 Onion, Sliced
- 1 Tbsp. Freshly Grated Ginger
- 1 Red Bell Pepper, Seeds Removed
- Sea Salt and Black Pepper
- Red Pepper Flakes (Depending on Spice Factor)
- 2 Cups Cauliflower Rice (Cooked)
- ½ Cup Chopped Green Onions (for Garnish)

INSTRUCTIONS:

Begin with a large saucepan (or wok if you have one) on high heat. Add 1 tbsp. coconut oil. Cook chicken until golden brown.

Remove chicken from saucepan and add remaining coconut oil and garlic.

Add all vegetables and ginger (except cauliflower rice).

Add Thai curry paste and fish sauce.

Add coconut cream and stir together.

Add chicken back in and cook for several more minutes until blended and heated.

Add salt and pepper, to taste.

Serve over cauliflower rice and garnish with red pepper flakes and green onions.

Bon Appétit!

Main Course

BROCCOLI AND CHEESE SOUP

INGREDIENTS:

- 2 Tbsp. Butter
- ¼ Cup White Onion, Chopped
- ¼ Cup Celery, Chopped
- 1 Garlic Clove, Minced
- 2 Cups Chicken Broth
- 1 Cup Broccoli, Chopped
- 1 Tbsp. Cream Cheese
- ¼ Cup Heavy Whipping Cream
- 1 Cup cheddar Cheese, Shredded
- 2 Slices Bacon (Crumbled)
- ½ Tsp. Xanthan Gum
- Sea Salt and Black Pepper, to Taste

INSTRUCTIONS:

Begin by heating a medium sized saucepan on medium heat.

Add butter, garlic, celery, onion, salt, and pepper. Cook until vegetables are translucent.

Add broccoli.

Add chicken broth, cream cheese and whipping cream and bring to a boil.

Turn down the temperature and add shredded cheese. Stir until completely melted.

Add xanthan gum and stir until soup thickens.

Add bacon crumbles and serve warm.

Bon Appétit!

Main Course

LOADED ZUCCHINI BOATS

INGREDIENTS:

- 6 Zucchini (Medium-Large Sized)
- 1 ½ Lb. Ground Beef
- 2 Garlic Cloves, Minced
- 1 Cup Tomatoes, Diced
- 4 Oz. Cream Cheese
- 1 Cup White Onion, Diced
- 1 Cup Baby Portobello Mushroom, Chopped
- ½ Cup Red Bell Pepper, Chopped
- ½ Cup Green Bell Pepper, Chopped
- 2 Cups Cheddar Cheese, Shredded
- Sea Salt and Black Pepper, to Taste
- 1 Tbsp. Italian Seasoning and/or Basil (Optional)

INSTRUCTIONS:

Preheat the oven to 350°F.

Cut the ends of the zucchini and then cut in half lengthwise. Scoop out the inside, leaving the shells.

In a medium size pan cook beef with ½ cup diced onion and minced garlic.

Add salt and pepper.

Once beef is thoroughly cooked, drain meat.

Add remaining onions, tomatoes, mushrooms, and red and green peppers.

Once vegetables have cooked, add cream cheese and 1 cup of shredded cheddar cheese.

Add salt and pepper, to taste.

Spoon mixture into zucchini shells.

Place zucchini shells into a pre-greased (avocado oil works well) baking dish.

Sprinkle remaining cheese evenly over the 12 zucchini boats. Option to add Italian seasoning and/or basil.

Bake for approximately 25-30 minutes, until zucchini is soft and tender.

Bon Appétit!

Main Course

BUFFALO CHICKEN MEATBALLS

INGREDIENTS:

- 1 Lb. Ground Chicken
- 1 Large Egg
- ½ Cup Almond Flour
- 4 Tbsp. Ranch Dressing (Pg.10)
- 1/3 Cup Celery, Finely Minced
- 1/3 Cup Carrots, Finely Minced
- 1 Clove Garlic, Minced
- Sea Salt and Black Pepper, to Taste
- 1/3 Cup Frank's Hot Sauce

INSTRUCTIONS:

Preheat oven to 400°F.

Line baking sheet with parchment paper.

Add all ingredients to a mixing bowl (including ground chicken).

Mix with hands (be careful not to over mix).

Form small round balls (about 1 ½ inch).

Bake for 15 minutes.

Serve with extra hot sauce and ranch dressing!

Bon Appétit!

Main Course

CHICKEN AND CHEESE STUFFED RED PEPPERS

INGREDIENTS:

- 1 Lb. Cooked Chicken (Shredded)
- 2 Tbsp. Avocado Oil
- 1 Cup Fresh Spinach, Chopped
- 2 Cups Sharp Cheddar Cheese, Shredded
- ½ Cup Monterey Jack Cheese, Shredded
- 1 Cup Tomatoes, Diced
- 8 Oz. Cream Cheese
- 4 Red Bell Peppers
- 2 Tbsp. Cumin
- Sea Salt and Black Pepper

INSTRUCTIONS:

Preheat oven to 350°F.

Begin preparing the pepper shells by cutting the bell peppers in half, lengthwise. Remove seeds. Sprinkle with 1 tbsp. avocado oil.

Use remaining oil to grease baking dish.

Mix remaining ingredients in a bowl.

Stuff peppers with mixture and sprinkle with additional salt and pepper.

Place in pre-greased baking dish and place in oven for 30 minutes.

Bon Appétit!

Main Course

CREAMY SUN-DRIED TOMATO CHICKEN

INGREDIENTS:

- 1 Lb. Chicken Breasts (Can Cut Into Strips)
- 1 Tbsp. Avocado Oil
- ¼ Chicken Broth
- 1 ½ Cup Heavy Cream
- ½ Cup Sun-Dried Tomatoes (Reserve Oil For Cooking with Chicken)
- 4 Garlic Cloves, Minced
- 3 Cups Fresh Spinach
- ½ Onion, Sliced
- 2 Tbsp. Butter
- ¼ Cup White Wine
- ½ Cup Parmesan Cheese, Grated
- Sea Salt and Black Pepper, to Taste
- 1 Tbsp. Fresh Parsley

INSTRUCTIONS:

Begin by seasoning your chicken with salt and pepper.

Heat a large skillet on the stovetop with the avocado oil and reserved oil from sun-dried tomatoes. Cook chicken until no longer pink in the middle. Remove chicken and set aside.

Add butter to the pan, heat on medium. Add garlic and onions. Allow cooking until browning occurs.

Add wine and sauté for 2 minutes, stirring frequently.

Add chicken broth and heavy cream.

Bring to a boil and then lower the heat. Cook for about 3 minutes. Add sun-dried tomatoes, spinach, Parmesan cheese, and salt and pepper.

Add chicken and continue cooking until all is well heated.

Plate and top with parsley.

Bon Appétit!

Main Course

PECAN CRUSTED FISH FILLET

INGREDIENTS:

- 4 Pieces of Fish (Flounder, Cod, etc.)
- 2 Eggs
- 1 Cup Pecans
- ¼ Cup Butter
- 2 Garlic Cloves, Minced
- Sea Salt and Black Pepper, to Taste
- 4 Lemon Wedges

INSTRUCTIONS:

Begin by placing pecans in food processor. Process until very fine.

Beat eggs in a medium-size bowl until smooth.

Salt and pepper each fillet and proceed to dip in egg and then lay in pecan grounds.

Once fish fillets have been fully covered in pecan grounds and place onto a plate.

Heat large pan on medium heat. Add butter and garlic and stir.

Once garlic begins to brown begin placing fillets in pan. Reduce heat to medium-low. Cook until pecans begin to brown on the pan-facing side of the fillet. Turn with a spatula and allow cooking until the other side is brown. To confirm fish is finished cooking, use a cooking thermometer. Inside of fish should be around 145 °F.

Remove from stove top and plate immediately.

Serve with lemon wedge.

Bon Appétit!

Main Course

COCONUT SHRIMP

INGREDIENTS:

- 1 Lb. Shrimp, Peeled and Deveined (Tails Left on)
- 2 Eggs
- 1 ½ Cups Unsweetened Shredded Coconut
- ½ Teaspoon Salt
- ½ Cup Coconut Flour
- ½ Cup Coconut Oil

INSTRUCTIONS:

Begin by taking a small bowl and mixing the flour and salt.

Beat the eggs in a separate bowl.

Pour the shredded coconut in a third bowl.

In a medium-sized saucepan, pour the coconut oil and heat on medium high.

Dip each shrimp into the eggs and then in the flour mixture.

After the shrimp are coated with the flour mixture, repeat dipping them in the eggs and then finally in the shredded coconut.

The oil should be hot by now.

Place each shrimp in the oil and cook until each side is browned to perfection (about 1-2 minutes on each side).

Serve with spicy mayo sauce (Pg. 9).

Bon Appétit!

Main Course

ALMOND CRUSTED CHICKEN

INSTRUCTIONS:

- 1 Lb. Chicken Strips
- 2 Tbsp. Avocado Oil
- 1 ¼ Cup Almonds (Ground in Food Processor)
- 2 Tbsp. Almond Flour
- 1 Tsp. Paprika
- 1 ½ Tsp. Salt
- Black Pepper
- 2 Eggs

INGREDIENTS:

Preheat oven to 450°F.

Place chicken on a cutting board and cover with plastic wrap. Pound with meat tenderizer a few times until meat is about ¼ inch thick.

Salt and pepper the chicken.

Beat eggs in a small bowl.

Combine ground almonds, almond flour, paprika, salt and pepper in a small bowl.

Prepare a baking sheet with avocado oil.

Proceed by using tongs to dip each chicken strip into the egg mixture and then into the almond mixture.

Place coated chicken tenders on an oiled baking sheet.

Bake in the oven for 15 minutes and then flip and continue baking for another 15 minutes.

Once complete, the almond flour breading should be crispy and brown.

Serve with Dijon mustard or Keto ranch (Pg. 10).

Bon Appétit!

Main Course

AVOCADO PECAN CHICKEN SALAD

INGREDIENTS:

- ½ Lb. Chicken Breasts (Cooked and Cut Into Cubes)
- 2/3 Cup Mayonnaise
- 1 Avocado
- ½ Cup Pecans, Chopped
- ¼ Cup Onion, Diced
- 1 Celery Stalk, Diced
- Sea Salt and Black Pepper, to Taste
- Iceberg Lettuce Cups or Romaine Lettuce Cups (To Serve Chicken Salad in)

INSTRUCTIONS:

In a blender, mix the mayonnaise and avocado.

Pour the avocado mixture into a bowl and add remaining ingredients.

Refrigerate chicken salad until cold (optional).

Place one large piece of lettuce on a plate and scoop chicken salad into the lettuce cup.

Serve and enjoy!

Bon Appétit!

Main Course

EGG ROLL IN A BOWL

INGREDIENTS:

- 2 Cups Cauliflower Rice (Pg.16)
- ½ Lb. Peeled and Deveined Shrimp
- 1 ½ Tbsp. Fish Sauce
- 3 Tbsp. Coconut Aminos
- 2 Tbsp. Erythritol
- ¼ Tsp. Cayenne Pepper
- 2 Tbsp. Fresh Lime Juice
- 2 Tbsp. Avocado Oil
- 2 Garlic Cloves, Minced.
- 2 Eggs, Lightly Beaten

INSTRUCTIONS:

In a small bowl combine the fish sauce, coconut aminos, cayenne and erythritol.

Heat avocado oil in a large saucepan (or wok). Add garlic and allow to sauté.

Add shrimp and cook thoroughly. Remove from pan and set aside.

Pour eggs into the pan and continue to stir. This is important, as you want to ensure they get scrambled but are still tender.

Pour in the mixed sauce and the shrimp into the egg pan. Stir until all is mixed well.

Add in prepared cauliflower rice and bean sprouts.

Add additional coconut aminos and/or lime juice if needed.

Serve warm (option to garnish with cilantro and fresh lime wedge).

Bon Appétit!

Main Course

FRIED PARMESAN TOMATOES

INGREDIENTS:

- 1/2 Cup Coconut Oil (Solid)
- 2 Eggs
- ¾ Cup Parmesan Cheese, Grated
- 2 Large Green or Yellow Tomatoes

INSTRUCTIONS:

Begin by slicing the tomatoes into ½ inch thin slices.

Heat ¼ cup coconut oil in a medium-sized saucepan.

Dip tomato slices into egg and then into Parmesan cheese until each slice is well coated.

Place coated tomato slices into oil.

Turn slices as they begin to brown on each side.

Serve immediately.

Bon Appétit!

Main Course

BRAISED CABBAGE & SAUSAGE

INGREDIENTS:

- 1 Lb. Italian Sausage Links
- 1 Large Cabbage
- 3 Strips of Raw Bacon
- ½ Cup Onion, Sliced
- 1 Garlic Clove, Chopped
- Sea Salt and Black Pepper, to Taste

INSTRUCTIONS:

Cook sausage on the stovetop. This allows the fat to be saved to use in the dish. Once finished cooking, remove sausage from pan and set aside.

Cut cabbage and remove the core. Cut into thin strips.

Chop bacon into small pieces and cook in the same pan used to cook the sausage.

Add onion and garlic and sauté.

Add sliced cabbage in batches to the stovetop.

Cook until cabbage is wilted and cooked down.

Add salt and pepper.

Add sausage back to the dish and cook until sausage is reheated.

Remove and serve immediately.

Bon Appétit!

Desserts

PUMPKIN SPICE FAT BOMBS

INGREDIENTS:

- 2/3 Cup Pumpkin Puree
- 8 Oz. Cream Cheese (Softened)
- 4 Tbs. Erythritol and 1 Additional Tbsp. for Coating
- 2 ½ Tbsp. Coconut Flour
- ½ Tsp. Cinnamon
- ¼ Tsp. Nutmeg
- 1 Tsp. Pumpkin Pie Spice
- ½ Tsp. Vanilla Extract
- 1/3 Cup Pecans, Walnuts or Pumpkin Seeds (Toasted Nuts/Seeds Optional)

INSTRUCTIONS:

Using a blender begin mixing the cream cheese and pumpkin puree on low.

Add coconut flour, 4 tbs. erythritol, nutmeg, vanilla extract, cinnamon, and pumpkin pie spice. Continue mixing until blended well.

In a food processor blend the seeds/nuts with 1 tbsp. erythritol until finely ground.

Line a baking sheet with parchment paper.

Place mixing bowl in the freezer for 10-15 minutes until mixture becomes easy to roll in individual balls. Proceed with making 1 ½ inch round balls.

Roll the pumpkin balls in the coating until covered.

Place finished balls on baking sheet.

Freeze for approximately 20 minutes before serving.

If not serving immediately, move from baking sheet to a covered container that can be put back in the freezer. A Ziploc bag works too!

Bon Appétit!

Desserts

CREAM CHEESE PEANUT BUTTER FAT BOMB

INGREDIENTS:

- ¾ Cup Natural Peanut Butter, Softened
- 2 Tbsp. Butter, Softened
- 4 Oz. Cream Cheese, Softened
- ¾ Cup Almond Flour (Finely Ground)
- 1 Tbsp. Lemon Juice
- 3 Tbsp. Swerve (Sweetener)
- 1 Cup Dark Chocolate Morsels (Minimum 70% Cocoa Solids)

INSTRUCTIONS:

In a medium bowl, combine the softened peanut butter, butter, and cream cheese. Mix until smooth.

Combine the swerve powder and erythritol. Mix vigorously.

Add almond flour, lemon juice and sweetener to the peanut butter-cream cheese mixture.

Place bowl of the mix in freezer allowing the dough to become firm (about 20 minutes).

Remove from freezer and roll dough into 1 ½ inch round balls.

Prepare a tray with parchment paper.

Heat chocolate morsels in the microwave for approximately 30 seconds.

Dip peanut butter cheesecake balls in chocolate so that about half is coated.

Place chocolate covered balls on a tray and place back in the freezer until chocolate hardens (approximately 20 minutes).

Serve immediately or place in a sealed container.

Bon Appétit!

Desserts

PECAN CHEESECAKE FAT BOMB MUFFINS

INGREDIENTS:

- 1 Cup Almond Flour
- 1 Tsp. Baking Powder
- ¼ Cup Butter, Melted
- ½ Cup Sukrin Gold (Brown Sugar Substitute)
- 1 Tsp. Ground Cinnamon
- ½ Cup Pecans, Chopped
- 1 Tsp. Vanilla Extract
- 4 Eggs
- 8 Oz. Cream Cheese (Cut Into Small Cubes)
- 1 Tsp. Salt

INSTRUCTIONS:

Preheat oven to 350°F.

Line a muffin tin with liners or grease the tin itself.

In a large bowl mix almond flour, baking powder, butter, Sukrin, cinnamon, pecans, and salt.

In a separate bowl whisk together the eggs and vanilla.

Add the egg mixture to the dry mixture and stir.

Pour mixture into muffin tin, filling each muffin about ¾ full.

Distribute cream cheese cubes evenly (about 2-3 per muffin). If you prefer to have the cream cheese mixed into the muffin instead of in cubes, just mix the cream cheese into the dry mixture when adding the egg mixture in.

Sprinkle additional Sukrin on top of each muffin before baking.

Bake for 20-25 minutes, until they are cooked thoroughly.

Let cool before serving.

Bon Appétit!

Desserts

PEANUT BUTTER ALMOND COOKIES

INGREDIENTS:

- 1 ½ Cup Creamy Peanut Butter (Keto Approved)
- 1 Tsp. Caramel Extract
- 1 ½ Cup Unsweetened Coconut Flakes
- 1 ½ Cup Almonds, Sliced
- 3 Cups Pork Rinds, Finely Crushed
- ½ Cup Erythritol

INSTRUCTIONS:

Line a large baking sheet with parchment paper.
Begin by creating the caramel sauce.
Heat a small saucepan on medium-high heat and add butter.
Cook butter until it becomes a golden brown.
Pour in heavy cream and stir until the two are mixed.
Lower heat and let simmer for a few minutes.
Add in erythritol and allow it to dissolve.
Add salt and stir well.
Caramel sauce should look and taste like caramel.
On low heat, begin adding peanut butter to caramel sauce.
Stir in the caramel extract.
Remove from heat.
In a food processor, pulse the coconut flakes and almonds.
Add coconut and almond mixture to sauce.
Add erythritol and pork rinds to caramel and peanut butter mixture.
Stir well.
Scoop mixture onto the lined baking sheet. Use a large spoon.
Refrigerate until firm (approximately 1 hour).
Best kept in the refrigerator.
Bon Appétit!

Desserts

NO-BAKE PEANUT BUTTER CARAMEL COOKIES

INGREDIENTS:

- 3/4 Cup Almond Flour
- 2 Oz Butter
- 1/4 Cup Swerve Icing Sugar Style
- 1/2 Cup Peanut Butter
- 1/2 Tsp Vanilla
- Topping - Caramel Sauce

INSTRUCTIONS:

Mix all the ingredients for the bars together and spread into a small 6-inch pan.

Use parchment paper to keep bars from sticking to pan.

Place pan in freezer and allow to set for at least one hour.

Remove from freezer and spread the caramel topping on top of the bars.

Refrigerate for at least an hour or two until topping and bars are solid.

Bon Appétit!

Desserts

SAUSAGE PUFF KETO FAT BOMB

INGREDIENTS:

- 1 Lb. Pork Sausage, Uncooked
- 1 Egg
- 1 Cup Finely Ground Nuts (Pecans, Almonds, Macadamia)
- 8 Oz. Sharp Cheddar Cheese
- ¼ Cup Grated Parmesan Cheese
- 1 Tbs. Butter
- 2 Tsp. Baking Powder
- Sea Salt and Black Pepper, To Taste

INSTRUCTIONS:

Preheat oven to 350°F.

Add all ingredients to a bowl and mix on low with an electric mixer.

Using a spoon, scoop out small 1 ½ inch round balls (recipe will yield approximately 20 balls).

Line baking sheet with parchment paper.

Place sausage balls on baking sheet and cook for 15-20 minutes until they are firm and starting to brown.

Serve immediately or store in the refrigerator for up to 5 days.

Bon Appétit!

www.ingramcontent.com/pod-product-compliance
Lightning Source LLC
Chambersburg PA
CBHW081417160426
42813CB00087B/1180